GENUKI

**U.K. and Ireland
Genealogy
on Internet**

by David Hawgood

**Published in 2000
(reprint 2001)**

**by David Hawgood
London**

and

**Federation of
Family History Societies
(Publications) Ltd
Bury, Lancashire**

GENUKI

U.K. and Ireland Genealogy on Internet, by David Hawgood.

This book is being published in two forms.

On-line web pages at **www.hawgood.co.uk/genuki/**

This printed book, being published jointly by:

Federation of Family History Societies (Publications) Ltd,
Units 15/16 Chesham Industrial Centre, Oram Street,
Bury, Lancashire BL9 6EN.

David Hawgood,
26 Cloister Road, Acton, London W3 0DE, England
www.hawgood.co.uk   email hawgood@one-name.org

Addresses for ordering:

Federation of Family History Societies (Publications) Ltd,
Units 15/16 Chesham Industrial Centre, Oram Street,
Bury, Lancashire BL9 6EN.
phone 0161 797 3843   fax 0161 797 3846
on-line bookshop   **www.familyhistorybooks.co.uk**
email orders@ffhs.co.uk

Family Tree Magazine,
61 Great Whyte, Ramsey, Huntingdon, Cambridgeshire PE17 1HL, England.
Phone 01487 814050   fax 01487 711361
www.family-tree.co.uk   email family-tree-magazine@mcmail.com

ISBN 1 86006 111 7

The author is pleased to acknowledge copyright in examples, which are short extracts from web pages. The source is given with the internet link and the name of the originator in the caption under each example, or with each group of examples from one source.

The author thanks those who have commented on a draft of this book: Brian Randell, Phil Stringer, Peter Christian, Brian Pears, Ruth Satterthwaite and Barbara Hawgood.

Many examples are from the GENUKI web pages. The author is contributing a royalty from sales of this book towards costs of GENUKI and other provision of free genealogical information on the Internet. The word GENUKI is a registered trade mark of GENUKI, a charitable trust, which can be contacted through the author of this book.

This book is dedicated to the originators and maintainers of GENUKI

Chapter 1. Introduction

GENUKI is a Genealogical information service on the World Wide Web for the United Kingdom and Ireland. The name is derived from GENealogy, U. K., Ireland.

GENUKI contains over 20,000 web pages of structured information. It contains links to web pages of other organisations, but it also contains a great deal of information itself - and all information within GENUKI is available free of charge. It contains articles, and lists of topics with descriptions. It contains indexes and transcripts of original records. This book gives examples of the types of information provided.

The GENUKI web pages are held on many different computers, and are maintained by many people. Usually there is one maintainer for each county. But to the user, it is not apparent where pages are held - that is the beauty of the World Wide Web. There are standards for the structure and layout of pages, so they all look similar, whoever maintains them.

The GENUKI home page is at **http://www.genuki.org.uk** with links from this leading to all the other information. For the remainder of this book, domain names starting **www** will be given without the **http://** in front, so the home page will be given as **www.genuki.org.uk** .

Links from GENUKI home page (illustration of home page is overleaf)

United Kingdom and Ireland
Enter this large collection of genealogical information pages for England, Ireland, Scotland, Wales, the Channel Islands and the Isle of Man
Clicking on either of those on the GENUKI home page leads to the same place, a page with a list of regions and a list of contents. From here you can follow the links down to the area or place of interest, then look for the appropriate topic.

The GENUKI home page provides other ways in to the structured information, as well as leading to some separate articles.

GENUKI Contents
Beware of contents pages! They just have a list of topics and links available on a page, without the description which tells you why they are useful. But this link is sometimes useful when you know a link exists, and it is also useful in that it leads to a search facility on **www.genuki.org.uk/search.html** .

Guidance for First-Time Users of these Pages
An article describing the structure of GENUKI, with links.

Guidance for Potential Contributors to these pages
An article with links to standards, and a plea for more contributors. See more about this at the end of Chapter 5 of this book.

Getting started in genealogy
A useful article with a few links, including some to further introductory articles:

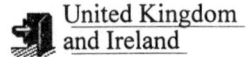 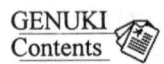
Guidance for
First-Time Users
of These Pages

**UK & Ireland
Genealogy**

Guidance for
Potential Contributors
to These Pages

Enter this large collection of genealogical information pages for England, Ireland, Scotland, Wales, the Channel Islands, and the Isle of Man.

Getting started in genealogy	Frequently Asked Questions (FAQs)	Researching UK and Irish genealogy from abroad
World genealogy, newsgroups and bulletin boards, etc.	Recent changes to these pages	Upcoming UK & Ireland Genealogical events (GENEVA)

To report errors found in these pages, please use this list of GENUKI maintainers in order to find the appropriate email address.

Note: The information provided by GENUKI must not be used for commercial purposes, and all specific restrictions concerning usage, copyright notices, etc., that are to be found on individual information pages within GENUKI must be strictly adhered to. Violation of these rules could gravely harm the cooperation that GENUKI is obtaining from many information providers, and hence threaten its whole future.

GENUKI Home Page at **www.genuki.org.uk**

A useful brief introduction, entitled "What is Genealogy", at **www.genuki.org.uk/gs/Bunting.html** originally produced for CompuServe, has been provided by Jeanne Bunting.

Another introductory account of British Isles genealogy and family history at **www.hmc.gov.uk/sheets/old_geneal6.htm** , complete with many useful references and addresses, is provided by the Royal Commission on Historic Manuscripts.

A yet more detailed on-line introduction is the A-Z of British Genealogical Research by Ashton Emery at **www.genuki.org.uk/big/EmeryPaper.html**

World genealogy, newsgroups and bulletin boards, etc.
A short article including links to the newsgroups soc.genealogy.britain and soc.genealogy.ireland also links to the main lists of newsgroups and mailing lists, genealogy portals and directories like Cyndislist - so this article has many links useful

in UK & Ireland Genealogy as well as world-wide genealogy.

Frequently Asked Questions (FAQs)
This leads to useful summary lists arranged by county, and text answers to questions. There is detail from this in Chapter 2.

Recent changes to these pages
This is a list with a new page each quarter, showing changes made to GENUKI pages. If you have used GENUKI before it is well worth a look, you may find major enhancements in counties of interest. For example the entry for 28 Jan 2000:

Cambridgeshire
• There is now a complete set of pages for Cambridgeshire Towns and Parishes.

Researching UK and Irish genealogy from abroad
A helpful article with useful links

Upcoming UK & Ireland Genealogical Events (GENEVA)
There is an extract from this calendar in example 6.3. It also has links to other web pages with calendars for particular societies.

List of GENUKI Maintainers
Please don't send them genealogy queries, but please do tell them about any errors and changed links you find on their pages.

Places and Topics: structure of the main material of GENUKI

Information is associated with geographic levels. The first level is information about the British Isles as a whole. The second level is for "regions" of England, Scotland, Wales, Ireland (Republic of Ireland and Northern Ireland), the Isle of Man, Channel Islands. The third level is for counties (or similar, e.g. islands). The fourth level is for towns and most parishes. Sometimes there is a fifth level, for parishes within a town. GENUKI uses the county structure existing before 1974; there were major changes in 1974/5, and others since.

The information is organised in the same way as the Family History Library Catalogue of the Church of Jesus Christ of Latter-Day Saints (the LDS Church). (This can be searched on-line at **www.familysearch.org** - choose "custom search".) It uses the same subject categories or topics. Examples are census, probate records, church records, societies, archives and libraries.

The web page for a particular geographical area has a list of places at the next level down, and a list of topics with descriptive text. There is a structure of topics at each level. For example we can have information about census:

• for the British Isles - see example 1.2
• for a region - see example 1.3 for the Channel Islands
• for a county or island - see example 1.4 for Jersey
• for a place or parish - see Example 4.8 for a complete index and transcript for 1851 in Llanblethian, Glamorgan, Wales.

LIST OF SUBJECT HEADINGS

This set of subject headings includes all those those found in the sections of the Family History Library Catalogue relating to the various major regions within the British Isles. (Following the practice in the Library's Research Guides, we have included a few "see under" entries to allow for differences in terminology on the two sides of the Atlantic.) Most of these entries are, we believe, self-explanatory. However if in doubt about the typical usage of a particular subject heading we would recommend checking how it is used in the Family History Library Catalogue.

- Almanacs
- Archives and Libraries
- Bibliography
- Biography
- Business and Commerce Records
- Cemeteries
- Census
- Chronology
- Church Directories
- Church History
- Church Records
- Civil Registration
- Colonization
- Correctional Institutions
- Court Records
- Description and Travel
- Directories
- Dwellings
- Emigration and Immigration
- Encyclopedias and Dictionaries
- Ethnology
- Folklore
- Gazetteers
- Genealogy
- Guardianship
- Handwriting
- Heraldry
- Historical Geography
- History
- Inventories, Registers, Catalogues
- Jewish History
- Jewish Records
- Land and Property
- Language and Languages
- Law and Legislation
- Manors
- Maps
- Medical Records
- Merchant Marine
- Migration, Internal
- Military History
- Military Records
- Minorities
- *(Monumental Inscriptions - see Cemeteries)*
- Names, Geographical
- Names, Personal
- Naturalization and Citizenship
- Newspapers
- Nobility
- Obituaries
- Occupations
- Officials and Employees
- Orphans and Orphanages
- *(Parish Registers - see Church Records)*
- Pensions
- Periodicals
- Politics and Government
- Poorhouses, Poor Law, etc.
- Population
- Postal and Shipping Guides
- Probate Records
- Public Records
- Religion and Religious Life
- Schools
- Social Life and Customs
- Societies
- Statistics
- Taxation
- Town Records
- Visitations, Heraldic
- *(Vital Records - see Civil Registration)*
- Voting Registers
- Yearbooks

Example 1.1 at www.genuki.org.uk/org/user.html#subjects - list of topics, prepared by Brian Randell

Information is not repeated across levels. In examples 1.2 to 1.4 there is background information about the census for the British Isles, very little at the regional level except to say that the Channel Islands are included with the census for England and Wales, then considerable detail about each census for Jersey.

At present there is a substantial list of topics at the British Isles, region and county level. The town/parish level is being added.

Example 1.1 shows the complete list of topics. This example, and others in the book, are taken from GENUKI pages, or pages found as a link from GENUKI. For each, the caption gives the web address of the page, **www.genuki.org.uk/org/user.html** in this case. Sometimes there is a location (anchor) within the page, adding **#subjects** in this example. There is an acknowledgment to the name of the person or organisation contributing or maintaining the information. The examples are generally short extracts of text and may not preserve the appearance of the originals.

There are instructions for reaching most examples from the home page, or from a major section like a region or county. To see the list of topics start at the GENUKI home page at **www.genuki.org.uk** and choose "Guidance for First Time Users". This leads to a page headed "How the information on this server is presented to the user". Example 1.1 is part of this.

Census

Using the 1881 British Census Indexes provides a detailed description of the indexes and gives full listings of the relationship and birthplace abbreviations used.

Ron Taylor's UK Census Finding Aids and Indexes. (These include lists of "stray" census entries, organised by county.)

The Victorian Census Project at Staffordshire University aims to computerise a number of source documents and related materials relating to Great Britain in the mid-nineteenth century.

A searchable database of places in the 1891 census. This covers England, Wales and the Isle of Man and returns the County, Registration District, Registration Sub-District, PRO Piece Number and LDS Film Number.

Example 1.2 at www.genuki.org.uk/big/#Census maintained by Phil Stringer and Brian Pears

Example 1.2 shows the census topic for the United Kingdom and Ireland. From the GENUKI home page choose "United Kingdom and Ireland" or click on the link "Enter this large collection of genealogical information pages for England, Ireland, Scotland, Wales, the Channel Islands, and the Isle of Man". This gives the main U.K. & Ireland page with a description, then a map, then a list of topics - click on "census".

Example 1.3 is an extract from the page for the Channel Islands (reached by clicking on its name, or the relevant area of an outline map, on the main United Kingdom & Ireland page). It shows the general format - a list of standard topics (in this case Bibliography, Census, Genealogy). There is a description for each, containing relevant links with comments about them. If the description becomes more than a few paragraphs it is put on its own web page, with a link to it.

Bibliography

Channel Islands Genealogy includes a surnames list compiled by John Fuller of the Channel Islands-related research interests of a number of Internet and CompuServe users and many useful links.
Books about the Channel Islands Part of Charles Picot's Pages - a book list of essential reading about the Islands

Census
Guernsey, Jersey, Alderney and Sark are included in the Census for England and Wales.

Genealogy
L.R. Burness. "Genealogical Research in the Channel Islands" The Genealogical Magazine (March 1978).
Research in the Channel Islands FAQs (Frequently Asked Questions). Civil Registration Details, Research Libraries and Family History Societies here - a growing site, includes links.
Channel Islands Family History: **Reading the Records**

Example 1.3 from http://user.itl.net/~glen/genuk ici.html Topics for the Channel Islands. Examples 1.3 to 1.5 are from GENUKI Channel Islands pages, maintained by Alex Glendinning

The "Census" topic for the Channel Islands in example 1.3 had one brief piece of information, that they are included with the census for England and Wales. But there is comprehensive information about the census for the individual islands. Example 1.4 shows the information about census for Jersey (to reach it, choose that island from the list on the Channel Islands page). For each census year it says what index exists, and where it can be found. Some are published and available in many libraries, some available in only one or two libraries. In this case none of the indexes are available on the Internet - but this information service tells you precisely what exists, and where to consult it.

Descriptions of places

Many county and parish pages have maps showing the location of the county within the region, or the parish within the county. If you have a place name but don't know the county, try the searchable database of places in the 1891 census or other gazetteers included in example 2.8.

The beginning of the web page for regions, countries, counties and many individual

> **Census**
>
> Jersey is included in the Census for England and Wales - taken every 10 years from 1841-1891. All have been indexed.
>
> **1841** (typed index by surname) and **1861** (full alphabetical transcript) presently only available in Jersey at the **Library of the Société Jersiaise** and the **CIFHS** Research Room.
>
> **1851**, **1871** and **1891** have been published - see About the Channel Islands FHS. Copies were sent to the British Library, the Society of Genealogists and the Public Record Office and have also been purchased by the LDS and various libraries around the world.
>
> **1881** available through the LDS Family History Centres worldwide,including our own The Jersey Family History Centre of the L.D.S. Church.
>
> The **1891** Census Index is now out of print but plans are in progress to publish a working index on CD in 1999 to celebrate the **21st Anniversary** of the **Channel Islands FHS.**
>
> During the Napoleonic Wars a census was taken of all the men available to defend the Island in the event of an invasion. More information at General Don's Militia Survey of 1815.

Example 1.4. http://user.itl.net/~glen/jersey.html#Census Census topic for Jersey

places has a description, mainly taken from historic reference books. Example 1.5 is the description of the Channel Islands.

Societies

One special case is the topic "Societies". This has links to the web pages of family history societies. These may themselves have lists of places, with information about the places. Buckinghamshire Genealogical Society and Cheshire FHS, for example, have information about each parish. North West Kent FHS has a West Kent Parish Gazetteer condensed from their published book of West Kent Sources. The pages for Societies may have similar information to that in the GENUKI pages, but in a different structure - for example Cambridgeshire FHS has a page on "Research in Cambridgeshire" with information and addresses for archives etc. It is always worth looking at both the GENUKI page and the relevant Society page.

"Genealogy" and "Names, Personal" as topics

The topic **genealogy** is used for information and links which are obviously useful to genealogists, but don't fit in to the other topics. Example 1.2 includes the topic **genealogy** for the Channel Islands. Example 2.5, contents for Ayrshire, shows mailing lists and look-ups under genealogy. Example 5.3 shows that the genealogy topic for Lincolnshire includes links to lists of convicts, the history of a prominent

The Channel Islands

[From the Harmsworth Encyclopedia,1909]

A group of small rocky islands off the North West coast of France, and 90 miles South of England. The group consists of Jersey and Guernsey, two or three smaller islands - Alderney, Sark and Herm - and various tiny islets of rock or seacrags. The total area is about 75 square miles. The soil is fertile and exceptionally well cultivated. The islands send large quantities of early potatoes, tomatoes, grapes, and other fruits and vegetables to the English markets. Each of the largest islands possesses its own peculiar race of cattle.

The people, who are of Norman descent, are industrious and fairly prosperous. Their numbers increased from 49,430 (excluding Alderney) in 1821 to 95,840 in 1901, giving at the latter date the great average density of 1,278 inhabitants to the square mile. The language of every-day intercourse is the Norman-French patois; of the popular assemblies, law courts, and churches, modern French. English, however, is taught in schools. The islands enjoy practically home rule. The chief executive officer in Jersey, and also in Guernsey and its dependencies, is the Lieutenant-Governor. The people are Protestants and the islands are attached to the diocese of Winchester.

Example 1.5 from http://user.itl.net/~glen/genukici.html Description of the Channel Islands

family, and a link to GenWeb which is a collaborative internet-based transcription and indexing project.

The topic **"names, personal"** also includes links to lists of names. Example 3.3 shows the "names, personal" topic for Stoke Damerel (which includes Devonport) in Devon. This has links to a trade directory, and to a list of bicycle licences - sometimes there is information available which just doesn't fit into the categories available!

Using your Web browser

When using GENUKI web pages you are likely to link to a variety of sites - surfing the Web. You need to know some facilities of your browser. It is worth making sure you know how to do these before spending time on-line. Use the help pages of your browser to find the methods. This section is intended to list some facilities you may find useful.

Back. If you are on a GENUKI page, buttons or links on the page will take you back to higher levels - e.g. from a topic to the page for the county, or region. If you link outside GENUKI, use the "Back" facility of your browser to return step by step to pages you have just been viewing. For example on Internet Explorer 5 (IE5) I can click on a left arrow on the toolbar, or press the Alt key and left arrow key together, or click on the View menu, then GoTo, then Back. Which of these are available depends on what I have made visible - using choices on the View menu. The more toolbars and similar you have visible, the less space there is for displaying information. It is worth experimenting to make sure your system has the control facilities you like to use, but leaves enough space for information from web pages.

History, Favorites, Bookmarks: Your browser will automatically keep a record of the addresses of pages you have visited, and if there is space it will keep the actual pages so you can view them again without connecting to the Internet. On my system, clicking the history button on the toolbar shows what I have viewed for the last 20 days, clicking the history button again hides it. Altering this setting, and the amount of space allocated, is part of Internet Options on the Tools menu. (You can also use that to clear the history, if you have accidentally visited sites you would rather forget). If there is a web address you want to keep longer than the 20 or so days of history, add it to "favorites" on Internet Explorer, "Bookmarks" on Netscape.

Disconnect and Refresh, Save and Copy: There may be a lot of information on one GENUKI page. You can disconnect while you read it or print it, then reconnect later. You may also want to "refresh" to make sure you have the latest version of a page. You can generally save the information from a page, for example using "save as" from a file menu; sometimes you will find that a page has been made read-only so it can be viewed and printed but not saved. You can also usually use the copy and paste facilities to select a part of a page, copy it, then paste it - for example into a word processor. You don't have to copy a whole page, just the small section of interest. When doing this, it is worth copying the web address and pasting that into the document with the information you obtained from it.

Page not found: if you try a web link from this book and your browser tells you it cannot be found, it has probably moved. Try getting to it by the logical route through GENUKI, from the home page or the appropriate region or county page. I have described the logical route for obtaining many examples in this book. I will try to keep web links up to date on the version of the book at **www.hawgood.co.uk/genuki/** - if one of these is wrong, please send an email to David Hawgood at David_Hawgood@Compuserve.com - and if you have found the new link please let me know.

Email from the web page

A link on a web page may have an email address preceded by "mailto:". If you click on one of these, your browser will open whatever email program is set as default, with a form for you to compose a message and send it.

Please don't email your genealogy queries to the GENUKI maintainers. It may be tempting to click on the name of the person who maintains a page - but they are using their spare time maintaining GENUKI, and may not have any left for answering queries (or even doing their own research!).

You will find many addresses of people who are inviting queries - for example, in surname lists. Give your message a meaningful subject, say where you got their email address, and put relevant forenames, dates and places. It helps to put surnames in CAPITALS - but don't use capitals for emphasis, they make the message difficult to read. Say where you live - they may be able to direct you to a library with more information.

Mailing Lists and Newsgroups

You will find many references to mailing lists and newsgroups. Both contain public email messages. For most of them, anyone can subscribe to the list, join the group. Any subscriber can send (post) a message which is available to all others, anyone can send a public or private reply. The messages are usually stored in an archive that anyone can search to see if the same question has been discussed before.

Popular lists may have tens or hundreds of messages per day. Usually you can choose to receive a batch of messages as one email, called a digest. Sometimes you can choose to receive just a list of subject lines and retrieve only those of interest.

Because of the volume of messages and number of recipients, there is a "netiquette" advising what to put in messages. For example: use a meaningful subject line; don't send HTML or attachments, just send text; when replying put a short quotation from the original message, but don't quote the complete message. There is a useful outline of netiquette by John Woodgate at **www.woodgate.org/FAQs/netiquette.html**

Individual mailing lists have their own information and advice which will be emailed to you when you subscribe. Read it, and keep it (among other things, it tells you how to leave the list, unsubscribe). Some lists invite surname queries, and have a set format for the subject line to include the surname. Others discourage surname queries. There is an introduction to mailing lists and newsgroups by Brian Randell in GENUKI at **www.cs.ncl.ac.uk/genuki/faq.html#mailing** and a link to descriptions of many lists in "Genealogy Resources on the Internet" pages maintained by John Fuller and Chris Gaunt at **http://users.aol.com/johnf14246/internet.html** .

For most newsgroups and some email lists there is a file of answers to "Frequently Asked Questions" (FAQs). See **www.woodgate.org/FAQs/** (again by John Woodgate) for links to many of these. That web site also has a list of professional researchers who discuss or accept commissions by email.

GENUKI was initially created in early 1995 to support a mailing list genuki-L which later split into two:
for GENBRIT-L see:
http://members.aol.com/gfsjohnf/gen_mail_country-unk.html#GENBRIT
for GENIRE-L see:
http://members.aol.com/gfsjohnf/gen_mail_country-unk.html#GENIRE

These two mailing lists are "gatewayed" with the newsgroups soc.genealogy.britain and soc.genealogy.ireland respectively. This means that you can either have all the messages sent to you from the mailing list, or else you can view the same messages in the newsgroup. There are many more mailing lists than newsgroups for genealogy.

Before you ask a question on a mailing list or newsgroup, see if you can find the answer already on a web page in GENUKI.

Chapter 2. How to find information using GENUKI

Annotated list of topics

For each region, county or parish/town there is an annotated list of topics at each level with substantial explanatory text, internal and external links, and a list of lower-level places (counties within region, places within county). Example 1.3 showed the entry about indexes to each census for Jersey, with similar information about each, and links to locations of indexes. In other cases there is a variety of information. Example 2.1 is an extract from the **emigration and immigration** topic at the highest geographic level, United Kingdom and Ireland. In this extract there are instructions for joining a mailing list about shipping, links to articles, and a link to an index.

Example 2.1. Annotated list of topics. Choose UK and Ireland from GENUKI's front page. This has a list of regions (with map of the British Isles), then an annotated list of topics. Choose Emigration and Immigration in this list. There is a link to a page with the substantial text for that topic: example 2.1 is an extract from that page.

United Kingdom and Ireland
Emigration and Immigration

The Ships List - a mailing list dedicated to the discussion of emigration, immigration, ports of entry and departure, ship descriptions and history, passenger lists and any other related topics. [Subscription instructions].

Marj Kohli has provided information about 19th century emigration to Canada (includes Emigrants Handbooks, ships lists, etc.) and about the emigration of children and young women to Canada from 1833-1939.

The Public Record Office of Victoria, Australia has provided an Index to Inward Overseas Passengers from Foreign Ports 1852-1859 (indexed by Surname).

Example 2.1, from www.genuki.org.uk/big/Emigration.html maintained by Brian Pears

Frequently Asked Questions - with answers!

1. How do Mailing Lists, Newsgroups and the Web differ?
2. What is GENUKI?
3. I'm new to genealogy. How do I begin?
4. Where is the place called <?????>
5. Is there a Family History Society for <?????> county?
6. Is there a Surnames List for <?????>?
7. Is there a Mailing List for <?????>?
8. How do I find the address of the Local Register Office for <?????>?
9. How can I obtain a copy of a birth/marriage/death certificate?
10. Where are the Parish Registers for <?????>?
11. Can you recommend a good genealogy book catalogue?
12. How can I prepare for a visit to the Public Record Office?
13. I don't have means of accessing the Web - how can I use GENUKI?
14. I can't find <?????> in GENUKI - can you help?

Example 2.2 from www.cs.ncl.ac.uk/genuki/faq.html by Brian Randell

Example 2.2 shows the top-level list of 'Frequently Asked Questions' (FAQ). To see this - and the answers with appropriate links - choose the button for Frequently Asked Questions on the front page of GENUKI.

1. Why are so few Devon parish registers available on microfilm?
2. Why is Devon's coverage in the IGI rather limited?
3. What Devon wills survive?
4. I can't find <?????> in GENUKI/Devon - can you help?
5. Is it worth joining the Devon Family History Society?
6. Does the Devon Family History Society have an email address?
7. I've just subscribed - is anyone researching the name <?????>?
8. Could some SKS look up the <?????> census for me?
9. What is the WCSL?
10. What is the Burnet Morris Index?
11. Where are the records for <?????> parish?
12. Where is Stoke Damerel?
13. Where is Devonport?
14. How can I contribute to GENUKI/Devon?
15. I have some photographs of <?????> church - would you like them for GENUKI/Devon?
16. Can I submit my GEDCOM file to GENUKI/Devon?
17. How do I unsubscribe from DEVON-L?
Other, more general, questions

Example 2.3 part 1 from www.cs.ncl.ac.uk/genuki/DEV/DevonFAQ.html -
Frequently Asked Questions, from GENUKI Devon pages by Brian Randell

There are FAQ lists reached from some county pages - eg the Devon FAQ in example 2.3 explains why you can't see microfilms of parish registers except in Devon record office, and how you can see information from Devon wills although the originals were destroyed by fire.

Newcomers to DEVON-L (and people who've mislaid their bookmarks!) frequently post queries that could be easily answered by reference to the World Wide Web-based UK & Ireland Genealogical Information Service (GENUKI), in particular to GENUKI/Devon.

The purpose of this "Devon FAQ file" is to give answers to the above queries, in many cases simply by reference to the appropriate section of GENUKI/Devon, i.e. of: www.cs.ncl.ac.uk/genuki /DEV/. (A copy of this FAQ file will be posted occasionally to DEVON-L, and also held in GENUKI, reachable directly from the GENUKI/Devon page, as the file is also intended to be of assistance to GENUKI/Devon users.)

Example 2.3 part 2 - explanation of purpose of FAQs of part 1

Example 2.4 is the answer to question 3 of example 2.3, and is on the same web page.

---

3. What Devon wills survive?

Prior to 1858, wills were proved in Devon in five main ecclesiastical courts: the Archdeaconry courts of Totnes, Barnstaple and Exeter; the Episcopal Consistory Court of Exeter, and the Episcopal Principal Registry of Exeter. All these probate records were destroyed by fire during World War II. Few had been abstracted beforehand, though indexes had been prepared for all except the Totnes wills. Luckily, the Public Record Office's files of Death Duty Registers (IR26 and 27) provide summaries of many but by no means all of the Devon wills that were proved during the period 1796 to 1903, including those destroyed in 1942. For further information see under Probate Records on the GENUKI/Devon page. However, a few Devon parishes came under the Archdeaconry of Cornwall; their wills, plus various other individual transcriptions and abstracts, survive - see the particular parish pages.

Example 2.4. Answer to a Frequently Asked Question - from the same web page as 2.3

Contents lists - and why you shouldn't use them

There is a structured Contents list for each region and county. There is a link to the contents page as one of the icons at the top of the region or county page. Example 2.5 is part of the list for Ayrshire. Before even looking at the list, note that you miss a lot if you look at the contents list which just lists topics and links, instead of the annotated page which describes them. But they can be very useful in moving quickly around GENUKI, particularly in sections you have used before.

- AYRSHIRE
  - o Description and Travel
    - Ayrshire Railways
    - Pigot's Directory for 1837
    - Ayrshire Web Sites
  - o Genealogy
    - Mailing Lists
    - Ayrshire Look-ups
  - o Languages and Language
    - A Scots Glossary
  - o Military History
    - Ayrshire Military History
      - Outline History - 21st Regiment of Foot
      - Ayrshire Yeomanry
      - Scottish National War Memorial
  - o Military Records
  - o Names, Personal
    - Ayrshire Surname Interests Database
    - Ayrshire GenWeb Page

Example 2.5. from www.genuki.org.uk/indexes/AYRcontents.html Contents list for Ayrshire, generated by Brian Pears from pages maintained by Iain Kerr

I will illustrate the reason for using the annotated page of topics rather than the contents by returning to example 1.3, the **census** topic within the **Jersey** page. Part of this says where you can see indexes to the 1841 and 1861 census for the island.

1841 (typed index by surname) and **1861** (full alphabetical transcript) presently only available in Jersey at the **Library of the Société Jersiaise** and the **CIFHS** Research Room.

Example 2.6 shows the corresponding part of the Jersey contents - part of the Channel Islands contents page. Contents pages have topics and links, so the **census** topic is shown, with a link to the **Library of the Société Jersiaise.** But if you just look at the contents page, you miss the crucial information that there are indexes to the 1841 and 1861 census.

Census

- Library of the Société Jersiaise
- The Jersey Family History Centre of the L.D.S. Church

Contents pages start with a notice reinforcing this advice.

Important:

i. **PLEASE DO NOT BOOKMARK OR LINK TO THIS PAGE** - this is just a summary of the **links** on the GENUKI pages relating to the Channel Islands. There is a lot of useful information on the Channel Islands page itself which is not detailed below.
ii. Material of relevance to the Channel Islands can also be found on the British Isles page and on the GENUKI Home page.

Example 2.6 from www.genuki.org.uk/indexes/CHIcontents.html GENUKI Contents page for the Channel Islands. GENUKI Contents pages are maintained by Brian Pears

Societies, Surname and email lists for all counties

- England
  o Bedfordshire
  o Berkshire
  o Buckinghamshire

Example 2.7 part 1, from www.cs.ncl.ac.uk/genuki/SurnamesList/ - links to lists for each county, maintained by Brian Randell

The structure of GENUKI goes down from larger to smaller geographic areas - country, county, parish - with topics appearing at all levels. There is generally no link for one topic across all counties, or at different levels. GENUKI does have a few lists arranged by county. There is a list of family history societies, one of surname lists, and one of email lists. The top-level FAQ is a good way in to these.

Example 2.7. Surname Lists . Click on Question 6 in example 2.2; . i.e from front page, choose Frequently Asked Questions, then choose surname lists.

SURNAME LISTS

This page brings together links to the listings that various people are compiling of Surnames being researched in the different counties, with the names and Internet email addresses of the researchers concerned. (Though these surname lists are not formally part of GENUKI, many of them have been set up in close co-operation with GENUKI, though others are quite independent. However, in either case comments and questions regarding any given list should be addressed to the maintainer of that particular list.)

At the foot of this page there is, in addition, a link to a list of (mainly) Fidonet users and the surnames they are researching in the UK and Ireland.

Volunteers are sought for the various counties that as yet do not have Surname Listings being compiled for them.

NOTE: Very useful though these online listings are, one should not neglect the very large and well-established listing (well over 100,000 entries), which though of worldwide scope is very largely concentrated on the UK and Ireland, provided in the annually-updated book (and occasional CD-ROM) *Genealogical Research Directory*, published by Keith Johnson and Malcolm Sainty. (Agents in 10 countries - British Agent: Mrs Elizabeth Simpson, 2 Stella Grove, Tollerton, Notts. NG12 4EY. Fax: (0115) 937 7018.)

Example 2.7 part 2, from www.cs.ncl.ac.uk/genuki/SurnamesList/ - explanation of lists, maintained by Brian Randell

Finding places and putting them on maps

Gazetteers

The Ordnance Survey have provided an online search facility for place-names occurring on their current Landranger 1:50000 maps. This covers England, Scotland and Wales.

A searchable database of places in the 1891 census covers England, Wales and the Isle of Man and returns the County, Registration District, Registration Sub-District, PRO Piece Number and LDS Film Number.

An online Parish Locator covering the whole of the UK. This includes facilities for listing other churches and parishes within any specified distance of the parish church.

Example 2.8 at www.genuki.org.uk/big/#Gazetteers maintained by Phil Stringer and Brian Pears. Web links are given in the next three examples.

There are ways of finding places if you have a place name but aren't sure of the county. Example 2.8 shows the Gazetteers section of the U.K. and Northern Ireland page with three different ways of searching by place name. All of these initially show a list of all places of that name, with counties. Some of them also produce maps.

There are maps you can display on your own web pages, or print for your own use.

Name	County	Description	Grid Reference	Landranger Sheet(s)	Latitude/ Longitude
Kemerton	Worcestershire	City, town, village, etc.	SO9437	150	52° 2.1' N 2° 4.8' W

Example 2.9, search result from
www.ordsvy.gov.uk/products/Landranger/lrmsearch.cfm on an Ordnance
Survey web page

The searches used for the examples are on villages around Kemerton (the author's birthplace). It was in Gloucestershire up to a local government reorganisation in the 1930s, then transferred to Worcestershire - so this is a place that appears in different counties on different gazetteers. Example 2.9 shows the result on a search for Kemerton on the Ordnance Survey Gazetteer. This shows the sheet of the Landranger map (1:50,000 scale) including the place, and clicking on the sheet number gives a diagram showing major towns on the sheet. The Ordnance Survey provides a service Get-a-map at **www.ordsvy.gov.uk/getamap/** which provides sections of maps at 1:250,000 scale. You can print these for your own use, or put up to ten of them on a website.

Example 2.10 shows the results of a search on the searchable database of places in the 1891 census. The county, district, sub-district and place names have links to the appropriate GENUKI pages.

County	District	Sub-District	Place	PRO piece number	LDS Film
Gloucestershire	Tewkesbury	Tewkesbury	Kemerton	RG12-2050	6097160

Example 2.10, search result from www.genuki.org.uk/big/census_place.html -
census place database on GENUKI pages maintained by Phil Stringer and Brian
Pears

Example 2.11 shows the result of a search on the Parish Locator looking for parishes up to 3 km from Kemerton, historically in Gloucestershire. Clicking on a grid reference from example 2.11 gives a modern map of the area from **http://uk8.multimap.com/** . You can link to these maps free of charge from your own web pages - they include advertisements which finance the service.

The links on county and place from the parish locator results go to the appropriate GENUKI pages. In this case there is a page for Kemerton - then in Gloucestershire - but none yet for the Worcestershire parishes. The page for Kemerton includes an

Km	Place	County	Gridref
2.2	Bredon	Worcestershire	SO920360
0.0	Kemerton	Gloucestershire	SO940370
1.0	Overbury	Worcestershire	SO950370
2.2	Bredons Norton	Worcestershire	SO930390

Example 2.11, result of a search on www.genuki.org.uk/big/parloc/search.html
by Phil Stringer from a database originally developed by Gerry Lawson

outline map, reproduced in Example 2.12, showing its location relative to major
towns. (Kemerton is the filled-in area protruding on the county boundary north of
Cheltenham. On the web page the parish is coloured red). There is an outline map
like this for each parish of Gloucestershire.

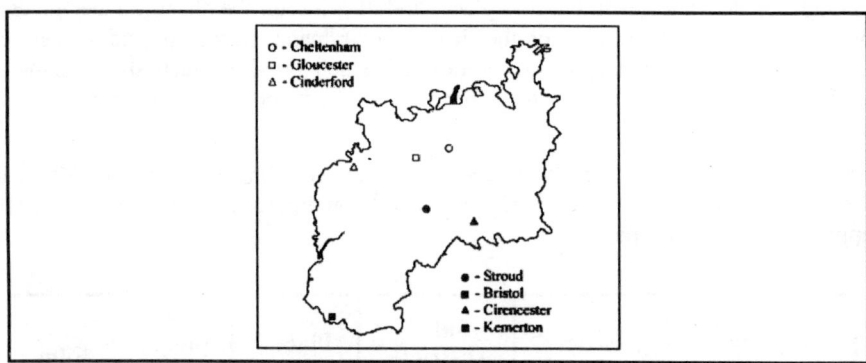

Example 2.12 map from www.genuki.org.uk/big/eng/GLS/Kemerton/ on the
GENUKI Gloucestershire pages maintained by Rosemary Lockie

Searches within GENUKI

There is a search facility covering all pages which are within GENUKI. It is at
www.genuki.org.uk/search.html (a link from the GENUKI home page is likely to
be added). If you are used to search engines like AltaVista, you will find the
GENUKI search rather different. When it finds a word it displays it in context, with
surrounding text from the first occurrence of a search word on the web page, rather
than just the description or first few sentences of the page.

There is a link to it on the main contents page of GENUKI.

For some counties (eg Devon, Durham) there is a search facility which operates over
most of the pages for that county.

Chapter 3. Indexes and Transcripts

GENUKI gives access to indexes of names and summaries of documents in a variety of ways. However you get them, remember that there is usually more information in the original document. An index to a marriage will just give the names of bride and groom; the register entry may give their ages, homes, occupations, whether they have been widowed, names of fathers, and names of witnesses. Once you have a reference to a document, you can usually get a copy quite cheaply from the archives holding the original. You can also employ a searcher to look at the original, get you a photocopy, and transcribe additional information. There is a list of professional researchers who discuss or accept commissions by email on John Woodgate's pages at **www.woodgate.org/FAQs/adverts.html** .

GENUKI may contain or have links to:

Transcript or abstract (in date or other original order of the document) as a web page.

Index (usually in alphabetic order of names) as a web page
See examples 3.1 to 3.5. Internet search engines work on indexes and transcripts held as web pages. You may need a browser "find" within the web page to find the entry. A search of GENUKI pages is available at **www.genuki.org.uk/search.html** .

On-line search of a database not on a web page
Notable examples are Scots Origins, FamilySearch, Commonwealth War Graves Commission. These have their own search, a "fill in a form" web page. They just return the hits, and entries are not found by web search engines. Example 3.6 shows a search of a database of passengers to Victoria, Australia.

Off-line search service: you pay a Family History Society or individual holding the index, to do a search. Usually payment and results are by post. See example 3.7, Northamptonshire FHS Personal Name Database.

Published Index to names: there are thousands of indexes available, mainly from family history societies, as booklets, or microfiche, or computer disks. Example 3.8 shows some marriage indexes available from Bristol and Avon Family History Society. The society also provides a search service. Most societies' web pages list publications available, some with on-line sales.

Abstracts

> **1794 edward playstead hungerford brk dean of sarum will comm cod 10350** will, codicil and commision of edward playstead 1) will of edward playstead of hungerford, chapman to my nephew francis bear of hungerford, cordwainer my freehold messuage in hungerford in which i now dwell and all my other messuages in hungerford etc to hold for ever but charged with a legacy of £20 to be paid to my neice martha bear of hungerford, spinster residue to francis bear who is sole executor dated 25 november 1783 sign edward playsteed witnesses: anthony woodroffe francis hahtridge wm deadman junior 2) codicil : revokes legacy of £20 to neice martha bear and gives legacy of £30 to great neice mary bear, daughter of my nephew francis bear (at age of 21 years) 23 march 1791 [testator makes mark] witnesses: richd fullbrook, jno: church, wm: deadman probate 28 october 1794 3) commision - the testator died 31 march 1791

Example 3.1. www.genuki.org.uk/big/eng/BRKwills/wa10350.html Abstracts of Berkshire Wills. Abstract prepared by Nick Hidden, and provided by him for publication within GENUKI.

Example 3.1 is an abstract of the text of wills. Nick Hidden abstracted the text of about 1000 wills from Berkshire and surrounding areas. They are wills for surnames of interest to him, but have other people mentioned - relatives, witnesses, executors, etc.. The one shown in the example is the will of Edward Playstead, but also mentions Francis and Martha Bear.

Transcripts of name lists

I found example 3.2 by using a search for "Blackmore" in the Devon pages of GENUKI. One hit was a Pigots Directory for Devonport. It gives the name, profession and address. The list is in alphabetical order of professions, then alphabetical order of names within each profession. The example shows just four names from the list, including the two "Blackmore" entries located by the web search.

Example 3.2 - heading

> **Name Listing from the Dock (Devonport) Section**
>
> **of a pre-1830 edition of**
>
> **Pigot's Directory**

Example 3.3 shows another way in to the same transcript by asking "what lists of names are there for Devonport?". To do this choose England, then Devon, then Stoke Damerel, then Personal Names. (Devonport is in the parish of Stoke Damerel - for

```
Berryman, Richd: Attorney            18 St Aubyn Street
Birkhead, R Hawker: Attorney         32 Chapel Street
Blackmore, Jn Pym: Attorney          50 Fore Street
Blackmore, Walter Pomery: Attorney 6 Morice Street
```

Example 3.2 from
www.cs.ncl.ac.uk/genuki/DEV/StokeDamerel/DevonportPigotPre1830.html
Extracted and reconstructed by Brian Randell from a file made available by
Cornwall Online - the Cornish Internet Magazine

ways of finding where places appear in GENUKI, see Chapter 2 examples 2.8 to
2.12).

Names, Personal

Devonport and Morice Town Names from a pre-1830 edition of Pigot's
Directory.

Devonport Bicycle Licenses - 1937-48, transcribed by the late Ted Wildy.

Example 3.3 from www.cs.ncl.ac.uk/genuki/DEV/StokeDamerel/ in the
GENUKI pages for Devon, prepared by Brian Randell

Parish Register Transcripts

Example 3.4 shows indexes and transcripts of church records for Durham. This is
under the topic "Church Records" in the page for the county of Durham.

Note that in looking for indexes you may have to look at different levels. At the top
level there is FamilySearch with the IGI including many parish registers, at the
county level there is a marriage index, at individual place level there are transcripts
for particular parishes.

I used the Durham parish register search facility from example 3.4 to search for the
surname Lilburn. One hit indicated was in marriages from Sunderland Registers
1830-1837; the first part of example 3.5 shows the head of this page. The entries are
in date order as in the original register. To locate the Lilburn entry that made the
page a hit, I used the web browser find facility to look for occurrences of the word
"Lilburn". The second part of example 3.5 shows a few entries from the register,
including that for William Lilburn marrying on 8th May 1830.

Church Records

- Detailed information on deposited registers and transcripts is given under individual parishes (see index below).
- Newcastle University have provided a search facility covering the parish register transcripts linked from the Durham parish pages, including all of those kindly supplied to GENUKI by George Bell.
- County Durham Burial Index 1813-1837 (5% Sample)
- Paul Joiner's Marriage Index for Durham and the North Riding of Yorkshire.
- Ted Wildy's UK Marriage witness index entries for Durham[ftp].
- Transcripts or indexes of about three hundred Northumberland and Durham parish registers are held in the Newcastle Local Studies Library.

Example 3.4 from
http://website.lineone.net/~pjoiner/genuki/DUR/#ChurchRecords maintained by
Paul Joiner

Example 3.5 pt 1 - page heading

Marriages from the Sunderland Registers (1830-1837)

This listing is produced from an index that was originally prepared by Bill Rounce and entered onto computer by George Bell with the assistance of Sandra (Hope) Bell. This index is one of a number kindly made available to GENUKI by George Bell from his large collection of Northumberland and Durham indexes.

```
5  May 1830 Samuel Doughty = Margaret Towell
5  May 1830 Joseph Potts = Grace Petty
8  May 1830 William Lilburn = Mary Robson
10 May 1830 Martin Mattinson = Cordelia Cook
16 May 1830 Daniel Bowan = Margaret Richardson
```

Example 3.5 from www.cs.ncl.ac.uk/~brian.randell/home.informal/Genealogy/ genuki/Transcriptions/DUR/SUN1830.html from a transcript by Bill Rounce, see acknowledgment at the start of the example. Maintained by Brian Pears.

On-line Search on database of names

The next example shows a link from GENUKI to a searchable database outside GENUKI - passengers to Victoria, Australia. In the topic "Emigration and immigration" at the top (UK & Ireland) level of GENUKI shown in example 2.1, we are told that "The Public Record Office of Victoria, Australia has provided an Index to Inward Overseas Passengers from Foreign Ports 1852-1859 (indexed by Surname)." Choosing this gives a choice of databases to search; the preamble to one of them is shown as the first part of example 3.6; the page continues with a form to fill in. I asked for entries for the surname "Excell" and was given the table of seven Excell

Example 3.6 - heading

Immigration to Victoria

British Ports 1852 - 1869

Index to Unassisted Inward Passenger Lists

You can search this index for names of unassisted passengers who boarded ships to Victoria from British ports between 1852 and 1869. Enter one or more of **Surname, Given names, Ship name, Year, Month** and the number of matches you require, then press **Search** .

Immigration to Victoria

British Ports 1852 - 1869

Index to Unassisted Inward Passenger Lists

Surname	Given names	Age	Month	Year	Ship	Fiche	Page
EXCELL	ANN	54	JUN	1857	ALGIERS	126	004
EXCELL	FANNY	18	JAN	1858	MAIDSTONE	140	001
EXCELL	HARRY	18	JUN	1857	ALGIERS	126	004
EXCELL	JAMES	29	MAY	1857	TRUE BRITON	124	002
EXCELL	SOPHIA	20	JAN	1858	MAIDSTONE	140	001
EXCELL	WILLIAM	24	APR	1853	JAMES L BOGERT	035	006
EXCELL	WILLIAM	24	APR	1855	ESSEX	091	002

Example 3.6. Result of search using www.cohsoft.com.au/cgi-bin/db/ship2.pl from the web site of the Public Record Office of Victoria, Australia

passengers shown in the second part of example 3.6. It is possible that the William on the ship Essex in 1855 is my wife's ancestor, and that Sophia and Fanny on the Maidstone in 1858 are two of his sisters. The microfiche reference may give me extra information to establish whether these are the right people.

Note that these Excell names do not appear on a web page, so they cannot be found using a web search engine. They can only be found by going to the relevant Public Record Office of Victoria web page and filling in a form on that web page. The information is supplied immediately from their computer, and is sent to yours.

Off-line search service

PERSONAL NAME DATABASE SEARCH

The Personal Name Database (PND) was started in 1993 as a joint project with the Northamptonshire Record Office as a service to readers trying to trace their ancestors. It comprises an index to a variety of material which can be found at the Record Office. It aims to record all entries in registers, extant in this county and instances of personal names in other documents, including the Christenings Registers from 1813, Militia List, Quarter Session Book. The information is held in the database under the following headings SURNAME; FORENAME; DATE or SOURCE.

Print outs are available at 50 pence Sterling to Members per sheet or at 70 pence Sterling to Non-Members per sheet.If the print-out is more than one sheet, this will be provided and you will be advised of the cost of the whole print-out.

Example 3.7 from www.crazydiamondcorp.demon.co.uk/nfhs/index.htm#search
on the web site of Northamptonshire Family History Society

Example 3.7 shows the description of a search service available from Northamptonshire Family History Society. They have an index on computer covering many different documents for Northamptonshire. The index is not available on the Internet, but you can write in and get a computer print-out of entries matching your requirements, at a reasonable price.

To find this page choose England, then Northamptonshire, then Societies, and Northamptonshire FHS from this; or choose the top level UK & Ireland, then Societies, then Northamptonshire FHS.

Published indexes of names

Bristol Marriages Index 1800 - 1837 (Microfiche)	
Part 1 - All Saints, Christchurch, St. Mary le Port, St. Nicholas, St. John the Baptist, St. Stephen, St. Werburgh	2.00
Part 2 - St. Augustine the Less, St. George Brandon Hill, St. Michael	2.00
Part 3 - St. Mary Redcliffe, St. Thomas, Temple	2.00
Part 4 - St. James	2.50
Part 5 - Society of Friends, St. Peter, Ss. Philip & Jacob, St. Philip - Holy Trinity	2.00
Part 6 - St. Paul	2.50
Part 7 - Bedminster	2.00

Example 3.8 from www.cix.co.uk/~kgroves/ba/pubfiche.html showing
publications available, from the web site of Bristol and Avon Family History
Society

There are thousands of indexes available for sale as publications, mainly from Family History Societies. Many societies sell their publications on line through GenFair at **www.genfair.com** , others sell by post. Example 3.8 shows the Bristol Marriages Index 1800-1837, some of the many indexes available from Bristol and Avon FHS. To see the list in GENUKI, choose England then Gloucestershire, go to the topic Societies and follow the link to Bristol & Avon FHS. Within that choose Publications. These are mainly large city parishes. If you know the parish you can get the set of microfiche for two pounds in most cases - postage about another pound - so this is an inexpensive way to get the microfiche index. But if you know you are looking in Bristol, but don't know which parish, you may do better with the search service shown in example 3.9 - for two pounds you get a search of all these 1800-1837 indexes and others back to 1754.

BRISTOL AND AVON MARRIAGE INDEXES

The Society has made indexes of marriages for all of the parishes in Bristol and Avon covering the period 1754 - 1837, with some earlier material for certain parishes and Quaker marriages. Send your enquiry for a particular marriage, giving as many clues as possible.

The normal charge is £2 for each individual marriage enquiry.

Example 3.9 - from www.cix.co.uk/~kgroves/ba/services.html showing services
available, from the web site of Bristol and Avon Family History Society

Chapter 4. Towns, places and parishes

In the geographical structure of GENUKI, there can be information about individual towns, places and parishes. This Chapter shows how to get to this information. It also gives examples of some types of information provided. For Aberdeenshire there is a list of parishes, a web page for each parish, an index of place names, a map of the county, and an active map (click on an area of the map to display the web page for that parish). Different county maintainers have chosen to give different types of information. Examples here are a census index, for Llanblethian in Glamorgan; a summary of records available, for Tewkesbury Abbey in Gloucestershire (there is a similar summary for each parish in Gloucestershire); and for Stoke Bruerne in Northamptonshire a reconstruction of families from a variety of records - provided as a link to the compiler's website, outside GENUKI.

The first emphasis in GENUKI has been getting information about each county. This is being extended to places within counties, but at present the coverage varies widely. Also note that some Family History Society web sites have substantial information about each place in their area; it is always worth looking at the relevant Society web page. For this it may be best to look at the list of societies within the individual county page in GENUKI. Sometimes these list local history societies, archaeological societies, and others not on the list of Family History Societies at the UK and Ireland level of GENUKI.

From County to Parish

ABERDEENSHIRE - Parishes

The index below reflects the way information is organised on these pages.
There is one page for each of the Church of Scotland parishes which existed around the year 1830.
If you don't know which parish you want, then start at the index of 5000 place names.

To aid with the geographical location, a map of the county (8 kbytes) is available.
If your browser works with Javascript (generally means Netscape 2.0 or Microsoft Internet Explorer 3.02 (or later)) then there is an active map (23 kbytes) which may be more useful.

Select a letter below to go directly to parishes starting with that letter

A B C D E F G H I K L M N O P R S T U

Example 4.1 (first part) from
www.urie.demon.co.uk/genuki/ABD/parishes.html in the GENUKI pages for
Aberdeenshire maintained by Dave Anderson

On each country or region page there is list of counties or islands. For most counties there are separate pages for each place or parish, and the county page gives a way of finding them. Example 4.1 shows the various ways from the Aberdeenshire page to its parishes. To reach it, choose Scotland, then Aberdeenshire, then at top of page click the button for "Aberdeenshire Towns and Parishes". There is also a link in the body of the Aberdeenshire page under "Names, Geographical".

Choosing **A** from the first part of example 4.1 goes to the relevant part of the same web page. The second part of example 4.1. shows part of this list of parishes starting with A.

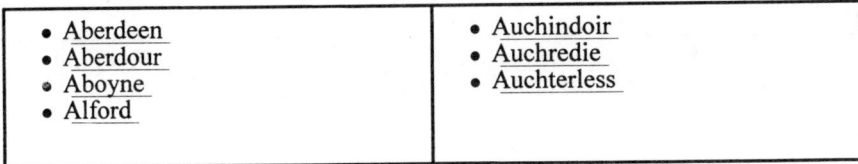

• Aberdeen • Aberdour • Aboyne • Alford	• Auchindoir • Auchredie • Auchterless

Example 4.1 (second part)

Example 4.2 is taken from the active map referred to in example 4.1. (The example is just a part of the image, without the active link).

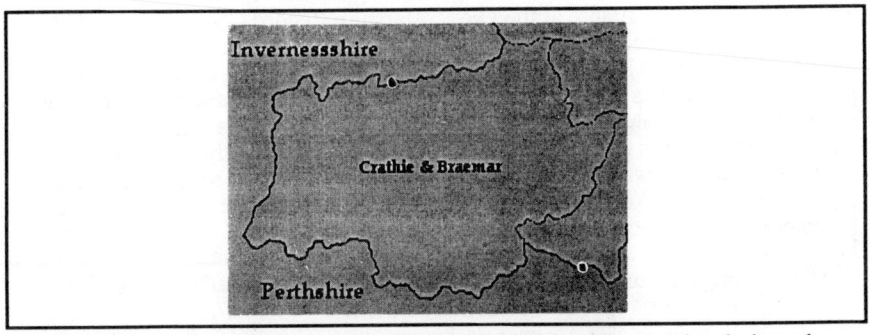

Example 4.2 www.urie.demon.co.uk/genuki/ABD/parishmap1.html gives the active map referred to in example 4.1, from GENUKI Aberdeenshire pages. The example is a small part of the map layout.

On the original web page, if you click anywhere within the parish, it gives a page starting as shown in example 4.3.

> # Crathie and Braemar
>
> ---
>
> **Contents of this page:**
>
> - Cemeteries
> - Church Records
> - Description
> - Maps
> - Names, Geographical
> - Taxation

Example 4.3 from www.urie.demon.co.uk/genuki/ABD/Crathie/index.html - Examples 4.1 to 4.3 are by Dave Anderson, GENUKI maintainer for Aberdeenshire

Information about records of a parish

The Gloucestershire GENUKI web pages have a summary of the records available for each parish. Example 4.4 introduces the summaries.

> Gloucestershire Towns and Parishes
>
> This Town and Parish List aims to cover all the parishes for which original source material is available at the Gloucestershire Record Office (GRO). The list may therefore include references to some parishes which are now in Herefordshire, Warwickshire, Wiltshire &c. Parish groupings, and spellings have been adopted as available in the GRO Handlist, but please be aware when consulting other sources that there may be considerable variation to what appears here, both in presentation and in spelling. Specifically, some parishes may have been known by quite different names in the past - for example, the modern day village known as Guiting Power can in some records be found as "Lower Guiting".

Example 4.4 from www.gen uki.org.uk/big/eng/GLS/Parishes.html by Rosemary Lockie

The entries for the individual parishes are compact tables with abbreviations for each source. It is advisable to look first at the introduction to the sources and list of abbreviations, in example 4.5. The same web page continues to give an explanation of each source. It might be helpful to print the page when looking at the summaries for Gloucestershire parishes.

Examples 4.6 is part of the same web page as 4.5. It is the description of one source, showing that "RMI" is "Roe's Marriage Index". The detailed description describes the index, and tells you where it is available.

The entry for each parish uses the abbreviations listed in example 4.5, which are

Example 4.5 from www.genuki.org.uk/big/eng/GLS/ROsummary.html

---

RMI:
Details of coverage in Eric Roe's "Brides and Grooms" - a Marriage Index.

These volumes are Gloucestershire's answer to the better known Boyd's Marriage Indexes. They represent in the main, an index to the Phillimore's Gloucestershire Marriage series (see above). There are separate volumes for Brides and for Grooms.

The volumes indicated are available on open shelves in the Gloucester Record Office. Copies are also available at the Society of Genealogists' Library, in London.

Example 4.6 from www.genuki.org.uk/big/eng/GLS/ROsummary.html

explained in entries like that of example 4.6, to summarise the records available. Example 4.7 is the summary of sources for Tewkesbury Abbey. For example it shows that registers of christenings from 1570 to 1847 are in the International Genealogical Index, with marriages from 1572 to 1850. RM/F and BM/F are microfilms of parish registers and Bishops Transcripts - available at Family History Centres of the LDS Church, so you can look at the detail for yourself. BIGLAND shows there are entries in the books of Ralph Bigland who visited many of Gloucestershire's graveyards in the late 18th Century, and recorded the contents of the Memorials. "Men and Armour" is in effect a list of able bodied men in Gloucestershire in 1608 - a militia list. Once you have had a quick look through the abbreviations, you realise there is a mass of useful information in the summaries.

Gloucestershire	Other Parishes	Previous Parish	Next Parish	GRO REF: 329

PARISH: Tewkesbury (Abbey: St Mary)	HUNDRED: Lower Tewkesbury
REGs: 1559-1958 **RM/F:** 1595-1853 **BTs:** 1570+ **BM/F:** 1570-1812	**Typescript:** **Printed Copy:** **IGI:** 1570-1847C 1572-1850M
RMI: B&G;1561-1808(X) **GMI:** GFHS: 1800-1837	**PHILLIMORE:** **BIGLAND:** Vol III,CCLXV **MEN & ARMour:** pp121-127 **TITHE AWARD:**
More information about this summary...	**MIs:** **War Mem:**

Please be aware that the information provided above is offered as a guide to your research only. Whilst every care has been taken to provide details which are as accurate as possible, changes and improvements in the services offered by Record Offices and Reference Libraries are likely at all times. Therefore if the exact details of parish record holdings are crucial to your visit, you are strongly advised to confirm this information with the appropriate office beforehand.

Example 4.7
www.genuki.org.uk/big/eng/GLS/Tewkesbury/ROAbbeyStMary.html
Examples 4.4 to 4.7 are by Rosemary Lockie, GENUKI maintainer for
Gloucestershire

Name list for one parish

In some cases there are complete transcripts or indexes of records for one place. Example 4.8 is the transcript and index for the 1851 census for the parish of Llanblethian in Glamorgan. I found the example by using the overall search of GENUKI at **www.genuki.org.uk/search.html** - putting in "Taylor" and "1851" and "census" as search terms. This is one of the pages found by the search. As the page is an alphabetical index of names followed by a transcript, I had to use the browser "find within the page" to find the entry of interest. The first search for "Taylor" within the page stopped on the alphabetical list entry showing there is a Taylor on folio 482. In this case I could continue to find the next "Taylor" which is in the household extract - for surnames which might occur as occupations (e.g. Brewer) or places (e.g. Cardiff) it might have been more convenient to search for the folio number "482".

This Taylor family came from Devon. It is worth noting that although "Payhembury" is spelt correctly, "Ailsbeer" is presumably the place in Devon spelt "Aylesbear" or "Aylesbeare". Searches on unusual place names can be powerful - but many place names are spelt wrongly in the census.

1851 Census for Llanblethian

Transcribed by Phil Mustoe

Format

Forename, Surname, Relationship to Head, Marital Status, Age, Profession, County of Birth, Place of Birth

Index

A List of Folio Numbers where each surname can be found

ADAM : folio 488, 489
ADAMS : folio 489

Ref:HO107/2461 f.482 p.21 s.90 Llanblethian

Thomas	TAYLOR	Head	Mar	35	Drainer/ Excavator	DEV	Ailsbeer
Mary	TAYLOR	Wife	Mar	45		DEV	Payhembury
Thomas	PENNINGTON		Unm	22	Drainer	DEV	Payhembury
Agnes	PENNINGTON		Unm	20	At Home	DEV	Payhembury
Jane	PENNINGTON		Unm	8	Scholar	DEV	Payhembury
Emma	TAYLOR	Daur	Unm	6	Scholar	DEV	Payhembury
Henry	TAYLOR	Son	Unm	9 Mon		GLA	Llanblethian
George	GREEN	Ldgr	Unm	31	Drainer	DEV	Landkey

Example 4.8 from www.genuki.org.uk/big/wal/GLA/Llanbleddian/ census.1851.html by Phil Mustoe, GENUKI maintainer for Glamorgan

Collected information for families in a parish

To show how GENUKI can turn up information you did not even dream existed, here are reconstituted families in Stoke Bruerne, Northamptonshire. Example 4.9 (in two parts) is the description of Stoke Bruerne in the GENUKI Northamptonshire pages, linking to Norman Tew's work which is published on his own web pages.

Norman Tew, who lives in Australia, has collated census and parish register information. If you have interests in that parish, his pages are invaluable. Even if you have no interests there, it is worth having a look at the pages, which show what can be done. Example 4.10 (in two parts) is from his opening page.

Stoke Bruerne

In 1902 a young pupil at the village school wrote a description of her home :

"It is a very pretty village situated in South Northamptonshire with a population of 400. The Grand Junction Canal runs straight through the village, it is specially interesting because of its locks and the tunnel, the boats have to be taken through the tunnel by means of a steam tug which goes from 5 am in the morning till 9 pm at night every two hours.

Example 4.9 (part 1) www.skynet.co.uk/genuki/big/eng/NTH/StokeBruerne/
(The above extract is from 'The Northamptonshire Village Book', compiled by the Northamptonshire Federation of Women's Institutes, published by Countryside Books, Newbury, Berkshire)

Description and Travel

The Grand Junction Canal is now the Grand Union Canal

Norman Tew, of Sydney, Australia, has produced the following transcripts and indexes, and is willing to share the results of his work with anyone contacting him by e-mail at normtew@localnet.com.au . He has also created a database of individuals contained in the Church Records and Censuses which can be found at the Stoke Bruerne Surnames Index.

Example 4.9 (part 2) by Maurice Kellner, GENUKI maintainer for Northamptonshire

Example 4.10, first part. This and 4.11,4.12 are by Norman Tew

Families and Individuals of Stoke Bruerne & Shutlanger Northamptonshire,England

There are 7301 individuals and 2223 families representing 872 surnames in this database.

The individuals here are from the censuses (1841-1891) and parish records of baptisms, marriages, and burials from 1700 to 1900. If you wish details of the records found for any individual please e-mail me. In some cases people may be linked to the wrong families, please e-mail me (see below) if you find errors. Thank you.

The names are shown in family groups.

Example 4.10 from www.geocities.com/Heartland/Plains/6222/sbn/index.htm

Example 4.10 continues to give an alphabetical choice of name indexes. I chose Index S-T, and went down this to the Taylor entries. A section is shown in example 4.11.

Taylor

Taylor, Thomas b.1870 - Shutlanger, Northants, England
Taylor, Thomas b.1852 -
Taylor, Tom b.1882 - Brentford, Middlesex, England
Taylor, Walter William b.1871 - Calverton, England

Example 4.11 from www.geocities.com/Heartland/Plains/6222/sbn/idt.htm by Norman Tew

Choosing Tom Taylor from example 4.11 gives his family, as shown in example 4.12. Tom Taylor was born in Brentford, Middlesex but by 1891 he was in Stoke Bruerne in rural Northamptonshire. An unusual progression? The description of the village gives a clue - Stoke Bruerne is on the Grand Union Canal (in fact there is now a canal museum). And where does the canal join the Thames - in Brentford! Use every clue when thinking how your ancestors might have migrated.

Tom Taylor [Parents] was born about 1882 in Brentford, Middlesex, England. He married Alice Louisa before 1904.

  CENSUS 1891. Stoke Bruerne, Northants. Fiche no. 6096298, page 2 no.9
  Age 8, Born in Middlesex, presumably a child of a former marriage.

  NOTE 1. This marriage is assumed from record of birth of a son to Tom Taylor.
  If this is the correct father then he was a labourer in Shutlanger in 1909.
  2. By 1914 the family were living in Bentley, Doncaster.

Alice Louisa was born before 1886. She married Tom Taylor before 1904.

  KNOWN from baptism of her son in 1909. She may be Alice Louisa Dyke born 1880

Example 4.12 www.geocities.com/Heartland/Plains/6222/sbn/pafg156.htm#380 by Norman Tew, examples 4.10 to 4.12 are published on his own web pages

Chapter 5.
Sharing, collaboration and surname searching

Genealogists collaborate in many ways. In some of these you can use the Internet to get in touch with others having the same research interests, to get answers to questions, to get people to look up books and documents on your behalf, and to search compilations of pedigrees sent in by others.

GENUKI provides links to these collaborations, but does not hold the lists and information. Example 5.1 is an extract from the description of GENUKI to explain this. To see it, from GENUKI home page, choose: Guidance for First-Time Users of These Pages.

In the main, the information that is provided in GENUKI relates to primary historical material, rather than material resulting from genealogists' ongoing research, such as GEDCOM files. (Its role is thus very different from Internet-based services such as GenServ, Roots Surname List, and the soc.genealogy.surnames.britain / soc.genealogy.surnames.ireland newsgroups with associated FAQ, that help genealogists find others researching the same family, and to exchange their research results with them.)

Example 5.1 from www.genuki.org.uk/org/ in a GENUKI page maintained by Phil Stringer

On email lists and newsgroups, you join the group (subscribe), and can then send in a question. It is seen by many helpful subscribers, and hopefully you get an answer. There are lists for geographical areas, and for special interests. Often the lists for surname queries are separate from the lists for more general queries.

In a look-up exchange, people send in lists of books, indexes and documents they own, or can readily search in repositories near them. Don't forget it is a collaboration - what can you offer in return?

Surname lists usually include a period and area where another family historian has research interests in the surname, with contact details. The list is either published or searchable. Some of the biggest lists, for example the Genealogical Research Directory (GRD) are published as books or microfiche or CDROM, not on the Internet.

There are large compilations of pedigrees sent in by genealogists and available on CDROM or on the Internet. There is information about these, and other ways of searching for surnames on the Internet, in the author's book *Internet for Genealogy*. The surname searching chapter is available at **www.hawgood.co.uk/finding.htm** . Also see Peter Christian's book *Finding Genealogy on the Internet*. The links from this are available at **www.walrus.dircon.co.uk/fgi/links.html** .

Surname and email lists by county

GENUKI has special pages with links to surnames lists and mailing lists, arranged by county. The way in to these has already been given in Example 2.2. From the GENUKI home page, click on the button for "Frequently Asked Questions". Two of these are:

6. Is there a Surnames List for <?????>?
7. Is there a Mailing List for <?????>?

These lead to lists for most counties - sometimes groups of counties. For example, the Gloucestershire Surname List has 14,000 entries. It is run by David Steel in South Australia. I looked for Excell and found two entries, with postal addresses (one in Gloucester, the other in Scotland). Following the link for Cornwall gives a surnames list, complete with location index, compiled by Jon Rees, of the Cornwall and Area-related research interests of a number of Internet and CompuServe users. Example 5.2 is an extract from this Cornwall Surnames List . In each case there is a place name, and a date, or range of dates.

PENGLASE St. Hiliary 1730s Shauna Hicks

PENHAL Godolphin C20 Jane Horwood

PENHALE Illogan 1836 Jon Rees
web address http://ourworld.compuserve.com/homepages/jon_rees/

PENHALIGON Truro 1860-1900 Barry P. Andrew

Example 5.2. from www.cs.ncl.ac.uk/genuki/SurnamesList/Cornwall/index.htm a Corwall surnames list compiled by John Rees. The original has contact email addresses.

More collaboration methods

Links to collaboration resources are also given within the individual county pages of GENUKI, and you may find a greater variety here than the email lists and surname lists reached from the GENUKI "Frequently Asked Questions". Example 5.3 shows the "Genealogy" topic in the Lincolnshire county page. To reach this, from the GENUKI home page choose U.K. and Ireland, then England, then Lincolnshire.

Look-up Exchange

Following the link from example 5.3 to the Lincolnshire Look-up exchange gives a clear explanation of the system, and encourages readers to support Family History Societies who produce many indexes. The first part of example 5.4 is the introduction, the second is an extract from the list of books and indexes on which look-ups are available from volunteers.

Genealogy

- The Lincolnshire Surnames List maintained by Nancy Clark. Lists many people researching various surnames in Lincolnshire, with the e-mail address of each researcher. An essential page to visit!
- Lincolnshire Genealogy Forum A good set of links for Lincolnshire genealogy.
- Lincolnshire Lookup Exchange A superb resource for on-line enquiries, this service is run by volunteers who will check certain indexes for requests. Well worth a look.
- ENG-LINCSGEN Mailing List Another essential resource for Lincolnshire researchers.
- Search Indexes and scroll of Lincolnshire convicts 1787 - 1840 Split alphabetically, these pages show Surname, First Name, Place of origin, Year of conviction and the Archive reference. Copies of the original document can be ordered using this reference.
- The history of the Guilliatt family in the UK and the United States This family has links with NE Lincolnshire.
- Researchers may be interested in the Lincolnshire GenWeb pages.

Example 5.3 from www.genuki.org.uk/big/eng/LIN/ in the GENUKI Lincolnshire pages, maintained (temporarily) by Brian Pears

Example 5.4

Lincolnshire Look-up Exchange

Many of the sources used for these lookups are the result of the dedication and hard work of a family history society. Many Family History Societies produce publications related to their county. You may want to consider purchasing your own copy of relevant resources to aid your research. Links to all known on-line publication lists can be found at Family History Society On-Line Catalogues. You may also wish to consider supporting research in this area by joining the society. Details can be found at their respective web-sites or see Genuki's Family History Society listings.

The following is a list of reference works on Lincolnshire which volunteers are willing to search for specific entries. To ask for a look-up, please click on the name by the reference. Requests should be specific: give as much detail as you can. Abuses of the kindness of these volunteers will probably cause them to withdraw their names so please don't ask for all references to a common name, or for time-consuming research. Volunteers may or may not be willing to obtain copies of the relevant pages. If they are, expect to reimburse expenses.

> **Oswton Ferry Cemetery MIs (dates between 1860-1991)** Stuart Moverly
>
> **Coningsby Cemetery Monumental Inscriptions 1885-1893** Nan Clark
>
> **Over 9000 surnames from Coningsby Parish Registers 1704-1968, including BDM's** Nan Clark
>
> **1851, 1871, 1881, 1891 Census Surname Indexes - some Horncastle, some Spilsby, some Boston.** Nan Clark
>
> **Horncastle Deanery Marriages - 1754-1812 (Vol. 19,part 1,2) and Horncastle Marriages 1813-1837 (Vol. 19)** Nan Clark

Example 5.4 from www.excel.net/~nclark/lincs.html maintained by Nan Clark
on her own web pages. Email addresses are in the original, but have been
removed from this example.

Surname interests of members of Family History Societies

Most Family History Societies publish lists of their members interests, so it is worth looking at the web pages for relevant societies. Some are lists of interests similar to those shown from the Cornwall surnames list in example 5.2. Others provide much more information. Dyfed Family History Society has collected pedigrees from members. Their web site includes details of marriages in those pedigrees, with year, county, name of groom, and name of bride. The membership number of the member submitting the pedigree is shown - both those in the example are from member 2329 - and the instructions say how to get either the email address or postal address of this member.

Example 5.5 From Great Britain & Ireland, choose Societies, and Wales within the page, into Dyfed FHS. This is **www.westwales.co.uk/dfhs/dfhs.htm** - at the bottom of this page is a door marked TAID (help desk menu). Clicking on this takes you to "The Advice and Information Desk" page **www.westwales.co.uk/dfhs/helpdesk.htm** which starts "This is a Dyfed FHS members' service but anyone interested in their ancestors, from the counties of Cardiganshire, Carmarthenshire, and Pembrokeshire, will find these pages of help."

Choose **Members' Ancestral Pages** from the panel (frame) on the left of the page.

I chose letter "A" from a menu and was shown the second part of example 5.5.

Example 5.5 part 1

Marriage Index

to Members' Dyfed Pedigrees

The entries are listed in surname sequence giving the full names of the marriage partners, county code and year of marriage. At least one of the partners was born in Dyfed or the marriage took place there. E-mail addresses, of members identified by their membership #, are accessible from the TAID menu. If no e-mail address is available then contact the Membership Secretary.

822	Anthony	Margaret	1799	CMN	Mansel	William
2329	Arthur	James	1865	PEM	Hicks	Eliza
2329	Arthur	William	1839	PEM	Davies	Anna

Example 5.5 part 2 from www.westwales.co.uk/dfhs/mpmindex.htm on Dyfed Family History Society web pages

GENUKI Supporters Club - free News and Comment

You may think that joining a GENUKI supporters club would entail mobbing the founders of GENUKI as they drive on an open-top bus through Manchester or Newcastle (to name two possibilities), but the truth is more prosaic. It is an open email list for news, suggestions and comments about GENUKI, or UK genealogy web pages in general. The method of joining is given on the web at **http://sentinel.mcc.ac.uk/mailman/listinfo/genuki-sc** . You won't be asked for money. GENUKI is free, and maintainers are volunteers.

You can help GENUKI to expand and keep up-to-date

The success of GENUKI comes from the large number of people who maintain pages now or have done in the past. And to continue the success it needs more people to contribute. You don't have to be a web publishing expert or run your own web site, if you can use a word processor you can help GENUKI. The requirement and background are explained in the page reached by choosing Guidance for Potential Contributors to These Pages from the GENUKI home page. The three parts of example 5.6 are extracts (edited to make the web addresses visible on the printed page).

GENUKI Help Wanted

There are a number of high level areas on the GENUKI pages marked **Job Vacancy** where we currently have pages with minimal information and no-one with direct responsibility for their development. We would like more volunteers to come forward to maintain these pages and preferably host them. More information about what this involves is available at www.genuki.org.uk/org/guide.html. If you want to volunteer or have more questions about adopting an area, then please contact Brian Randell (email Brian.Randell@newcastle.ac.uk) or Phil Stringer via his web page at http://sentinel.mcc.ac.uk/~zzassps/

Example 5.6 part 1 at www.genuki.org.uk/org/helpus.html

GENUKI is hosted and maintained by a number of people each looking after their own section but producing pages with a common structure and "look and feel". This means that browsers of the pages can easily find their way around and locate the information they want rather like you do in a library. We achieve this by having a set of standards at at www.genuki.org.uk/org/standards.html. which we all agree to follow. There are also a number of people willing to help and offer advice on producing WWW pages for GENUKI.

Example 5.6 part 2

If you want to provide additional information for an area of GENUKI that already has a maintainer then please contact them directly. The maintainers of each county can be seen on the information providers page at www.genuki.org.uk/org/providers.html . We don't just need people to take on whole counties in GENUKI, we need volunteers to develop more parish pages and to provide more topic pages (detailed guidance on a particular subject) for all levels of GENUKI (national, down to county and parish) - see www.genuki.org.uk/org/guide.html . If you think you can help, if you have local knowledge which you could share with others, or if you can think of something that would be a useful addition to the pages, please contact the relevant maintainer. Original transcriptions of local source material such as Census Returns or Parish Registers are always welcome, provided that any required permissions have been obtained.

Example 5.6 part 3

Chapter 6. Family History Societies

GENUKI has links to Societies. From the U.K and Ireland page, choose the topic Societies. This links to **www.cs.ncl.ac.uk/genuki/Societies/** which gives a list of family history societies. There is a page for each country, and a list of specialist societies like those for particular religions. There are also links from the Societies topic in each county of GENUKI. These give the appropriate family history societies, and may also give some local history, archaeology etc. societies.

It is always worth looking at the website of the appropriate society, as well as the GENUKI pages for the county and place of interest. Sometimes they are well integrated - you may find the Society page maintained by the same person as the GENUKI page. But sometimes the Society page has information which you would have expected to be on the GENUKI pages.

As well as looking at societies for areas you are researching, it is always worth looking at the website of a society in the area where you live. You will find meetings, courses, family history fairs, bookshops, often a library with reference books and the opportunity to borrow journals of other societies. And if you want to help with transcribing and indexing projects, it may be more convenient to help your local society.

What Societies offer

Example 6.1 opposite shows the topics on the front page of the Gloucestershire Family History Society site. The page also has a map showing the location of Gloucestershire within England. Most societies have a variety of indexes, produced over the years by their members. Often you can either purchase appropriate parts of the index, or have the society perform a search for you. This has been described in the Transcripts and Indexes Chapter, for Bristol and Avon FHS, see example 3.8.

The Gloucestershire FHS gives information about indexes, but not the information in the index. Example 6.2 shows the different approach of the Jewish Genealogy Society of Great Britain. This starts by inviting the reader to search the site by surname or town, or to try the Family Finder.

Want a quick start on this site?

- Try Search our Site and type in a surname or town name of interest.
- To trace recent deaths, look at Jewish Chronicle Indexes to Death Announcements 1995-1998.
- To navigate the genealogical internet, visit Useful Links and Information Sources
- Browse the JGSGB Family Finder Index Page

Example 6.2 from www.jgsgb.ort.org/ - web pages of the Jewish Genealogy Society of Great Britain

```
┌─────────────────────────────────────────────────────────────────┐
│                                                                   │
│      GLOUCESTERSHIRE FAMILY HISTORY SOCIETY (GFHS)                │
│                                                                   │
│   Registered Charity No. 296959 - (The Society is a Member of the Federation of Family History Societies.) │
│                                                                   │
│   QUICK REFERENCE                                                 │
│   1851 Census Index                                               │
│   Burial and Memorial Sites Index                                 │
│   Electoral Roll Index                                            │
│   Full index of GFHS publications.                                │
│   Gloucestershire Surnames List                                   │
│   How to join                                                     │
│   Items from the GFHS Journal                                     │
│   Marriage Index                                                  │
│   Memorial Inscriptions Index                                     │
│   National Burial Index                                           │
│   Officers                                                        │
│   Overseers of Poor Papers - Name index.                          │
│   Prisoner Registers Index                                        │
│   Resource Centre                                                 │
│   Search Services                                                 │
│   Strays Index                                                    │
│                                                                   │
└─────────────────────────────────────────────────────────────────┘
```

Example 6.1 from www.cix.co.uk/~rd/GENUKI/gfhs.htm - Gloucestershire
FHS web pages maintained by Ron Downing

Fairs and lectures - calendars of events

Most Societies have lists of their own events on their web sites. GENUKI also has
a diary of events, intended for open days, conferences, courses, fairs, etc. Example
6.3 shows an extract from GENEVA, The GENUKI diary of GENealogical EVents
and Activities.

```
┌─────────────────────────────────────────────────────────────────┐
│                                                                   │
│   October  15 Cheltenham, GLS      Family History Fair            │
│   October  21 Kidlington, OXF      Oxfordshire FHS Open Day       │
│   October  28 Doncaster, WRY       Millennium Family History Day  │
│                                                                   │
└─────────────────────────────────────────────────────────────────┘
```

Example 6.3 from http://users.ox.ac.uk/~malcolm/genuki/geneva/ maintained
by Malcolm Austen on GENUKI pages (these dates are in the year 2000)

There are many lectures and courses in family history run by local education
authorities and by societies. As an example of courses available, example 6.4 is a
description of the Institute for Heraldic and Genealogical Studies, which provides
courses both at Canterbury and by correspondence. It is followed by an extract from
their list of courses.

Example 6.4 (from heading)

The Institute of Heraldic and Genealogical Studies is an independent educational, charitable trust established in Canterbury in 1961 to provide full academic facilities for those who wish to acquire skills in family history research and subjects auxiliary to history. Day and residential courses at several levels are organised throughout the year. Part-time and tutorial courses by correspondence are also available and accredited.

Nonconformity	Day School	13 May
Tracing your Family History	Residential Course	24-28 July
Tracing your Family History	Residential Course	7-11 August
Parish Chest	Day School	14 October
House History	Residential Course	17-19 November

Example 6.4 from www.ihgs.ac.uk/ from calendar on web pages of The Institute of Heraldic and Genealogical Studies (dates are in the year 2000).

Society projects to index records

Most societies are active in transcribing and indexing records in their area. Some of these are published as national co-operative projects - the indexing of the 1881 census in conjunction with the Church of Latter-Day Saints of Jesus Christ is the most notable example. The National Burial Index in preparation is another - you will find that some societies provide access to their part of it, the first edition of a national index will be published in 2000. Starting in the 1970s, most societies have indexed major parts of the 1851 census; the results of this are published or made available by the individual societies. Another project which was agreed nationally but pursued locally is the recording of memorial inscriptions; most societies have a continuing programme of recording inscriptions. This is included as one of the Berkshire Family History Society projects shown in example 6.5. They also have a project to index Poor Law records. There is an enormous amount of information available in these; indexing will help all family historians.

The following Projects are in progress:

- Recording headstones and inscriptions in Berkshire churchyards and cemeteries.
- Computerisation of Society Records.
- Calendaring, indexing and publishing the Berkshire Overseers Records, that is those of the Old Poor Law, prior to 1834.
- An annual one-day conference when members with Berkshire interests gather from all over the country.

Example 6.5 from www.berksfhs.org.uk/ - web pages of Berkshire Family History Society

Help with your family history

I will end this book by showing the co-operation and help available through societies. Example 6.6 shows how Essex Society for Family History offer help. Sometimes this type of help is publicised to members of a society, here it is more public.

Do you need some assistance with your Family History?

Free general advice and help, especially for beginners who wish to trace their ancestry can be obtained by writing to the Secretary enclosing a stamped and addressed envelope or by sending an e-mail.

The following people have specialist knowledge of the subjects shown below which they are prepared to share with other members.

Example 6.6 at www.genuki.org.uk/big/eng/ESS/efhs/helpfh.htm#Family from the web pages of Essex Society for Family History.

I have removed the names and emails of the people offering help from the example - they change over time. But to give an idea of the scope, they offer help on General Enquiries, Monumental Inscriptions, and Roman Catholic questions for Essex. There is also help from different people with knowledge of specific areas of the county: Broomfield, Chelmsford, Chignal St James, Great Baddow, Harlow, Ilford area.

I hope this book will help you to obtain assistance with your family history, from GENUKI and from societies. Happy hunting!

Appendix. Format and amendments

This Appendix explains the format of this book, the relationship between the on-line book and the printed book, and will be used for any minor amendments if the book is reprinted.

There is a web page per Chapter. Each Chapter has explanatory text written by David Hawgood, and examples from web pages which are either within GENUKI or easily reached from GENUKI. In the printed book examples may not be immediately adjacent to the text describing them.

Examples are numbered within the Chapter. The caption under an example or group of examples has a link to the web page of which the example is an extract. There is also an acknowledgment to the author or publisher of the web page.

The actual example will be a short extract, sufficient to show the type of information available. It will be reformatted as text (monospaced where needed) with headings.

Web addresses whose domain names start with **www** are given without adding http:// in front. Thus http://www.genuki.org.uk is given as **www.genuki.org.uk** . Web addresses given may include a slash (/) at the end. Final full stops and commas are not part of web addresses, they are punctuation of the sentence. In this book there is a space between a web address and following punctuation.

The index includes subjects included in the text of the book, and the authors of web pages used for examples, but not the content of the examples.

The examples were copied from web pages in a period from September 1999 to March 2000. Those examples will remain in both the on-line and printed versions of the book, even if the pages from which they were copied change; they are intended as examples of the type of information available. To use specific information in the examples, please look at the current version of the web page; links are printed for all examples, and provided in the on-line version of the book at: **www.hawgood.co.uk/genuki/**

On page 9, last paragraph, the reference to Example 1.2 should be to Example 1.3. On page 13, first paragraph, and on page 16, between the two figures, the reference to example 1.3 should be to example 1.4.

The content and links for some examples have changed. Please see the on-line version of the book at www.hawgood.co.uk/genuki/ for up-to-date links. Please advise me by email to hawgood@one-name.org if links from the on-line version of the book do not work - I usually update links within a few days of hearing that they have changed.

Index